Hear
Haiku

Lawrence Eyre

Heartland Haiku

Lawrence Eyre

Published by 1st World Publishing
P.O. Box 2211, Fairfi eld, Iowa 52556
tel: 641-209-5000 • fax: 866-440-5234
web: www.1stworldpublishing.com

First Edition
Library of Congress Cataloging-in-Publication Data
Softcover ISBN: 978-1-4218-3628-7

Introduction

In these Twitter times
Haiku length may match people's
Full attention span

Postage-stamp portraits
Prairie psalms and proverbs make
Appearances here

Feel free to sample
Or stay as long as you please
You're always welcome

Heartland Haiku

If trees are giving
Their lives for this I'd better
Say something worthwhile

Father of Waters
You flow through simple songs of
Heartland prairie light

Find your voice they said
I'm finding mine as many
Voices go silent

Threescore years and ten
Sounds ponderous but it feels
Surprisingly light

Yesterday I taught
Tennis in withering heat
Today it's sweatshirts

Around here seasons
Don't slide they slam into new
Gears without the grease

Here is the heartland
Sewn together with silver
Mississippi thread

Bragging felonies
Carry lifetime sentences
In heartland justice

Let someone else claim
Straightest rows in the county
Are found on your farm

An eagle above
Father of Waters sees all
The places I've lived

Great-grandfather farmed
Grandpa and Dad worked for Deere
I teach what I've learned

That brick school wall took
Every match but it gave me
The game of tennis

Yale's yes plus fifty
Years back home ripened me for
This haiku harvest

Poetry purists
Might term these verses senryu
But that's too highbrow

These poems hitched to
Hay wagons pull us to a
Five seven five beat

Father of Waters
Quiet excitement grows as
We near your valley

Why do cars speed past
Sacred confluence of Rock
And Mississippi

At the edges of
Time our senses clarify
And the world stands still

In nature the high
Treble of eternity
Calls us each by name

Our deepest feelings
Surface now in sacred psalms
Sung from the heartland

Wisdom harvested
From lifelong learning gives grist
For heartland proverbs

Allure of limelight
Lessens God's good children turn
To stars in the sky

Whenever I see
Pleiades on an evening
Walk I know I'm home

In the fall extra
Dimensions crack life open
And rearrange us

I think we are not
Alone in this world or next
One life links us all

Life lived long means more
Memories no wonder old
Folks sift silently

Lindbergh flew across
The Atlantic the same year
Our Mother was born

Longevity does
Not go unpunished Mom's friends
All died years ago

Lifespan orbits start
Small grow global then shrink back
To where they began

We know what's coming
But open hearts say yes to
Full throttle finish

Some brilliant people
Think we're temporarily
Animated meat

But what if we are
Really *anima* that's meat
Temporarily

Anima is soul
Our deepest layer doesn't
Die it stays awake

Sometimes this haiku
Stuff strains my brain let's all go
Eat a big pizza

Old folks unfazed by
Tragedy have often earned
Their calm the hard way

Panda eye rings haunt
Chalky face gasping mouth locks
Open hands turn cold

Fantasy fiction
To claim we don't get cut to
The quick when lives end

Cry it's over and
Smile it happened honest life
Honors joy and tears

Life transmutes sadness
Into compassion when our
Hearts rest in wholeness

People fight unseen
Foes we learn about only
When the bruises show

Listen to her please
Truth hidden deep within will
Help to heal us all

Soliloquies of
Seventeen syllables are
Sometimes spoken here

If something's better
Than a crumble top apple
Pie I don't know what

Father of Waters
Southbound trains snake along your
Banks in a dark mist

Do trees sense their length
Of days many people do
Metering their years

Our lives all contain
Many deaths we dive through each
Wave and keep growing

A Mother's grief at
The loss of her child is deep
Beyond description

Father of Waters
You buoy our spirits even
In times of farewell

Fall does bring death but
Seeds of spring sleeping now will
Resurrect these fields

Truck tires shatter ice
Shards fly from roadway puddles
Frozen here last night

It's cold but we count
Blessings those loud geese left and
Silence filled the gap

Life piles up and soon
We've got layers stacked like cord
Wood at Christmas time

Babe in a manger
Infinity in a point
Angels heard on high

Our Mom smiled faintly
At the little girl in the
Old Christmas photo

May kindness given
And received overflow your
Cup this coming year

Life won't fit neatly
On calendars new carries
Old year's remainder

Heartlanders read most
In the winter while land sleeps
We wake up our minds

Robert Penn Warren
Taught Yalies a book's first words
Tell the whole story

Call me Ishmael
Bible folks know now how this
Whale of a tale ends

I umpire college
Tennis great seats but who likes
To get hollered at

After umpiring
We joke who is worst ump in
History this week

My brother Pat threw
A dart that stuck in my head
So that explains it

That's enough small talk
I'm just stalling because it's
So blasted cold out

Father of Waters
As you freeze brown barges plow
Shallow ice furrows

On a dare Dad drove
A Model A Ford across
Mississippi glass

Horses snort arctic
Air in turn lane while Amish
Driver hand-signals

Bitter cold proves life
Is found in layers long johns
Sold out weeks ago

Prompted by nothing
In particular these words
Keep tumbling forward

Dimensions collapse
In whiteout world only roar
And stinging wind stay

We interrupt your
Shoveling for this winter
Storm advisory

Walk humbly in fierce
Winds we do not own this place
Small steps bring us home

Father of Waters
Your flowing white robe stretches
Far as eye can see

At Yale they laughed when
I noticed snow fell straight down
Here straight in your face

Satisfying sounds
Shovels scrape sidewalks so clean
Then it snows again

Lone tree leaned against
The north wind for years until
A storm snapped it off

Scintillating snow
Brings a celestial sparkle
To this frozen zone

Child's winter wisdom
Finds annual audience
Don't eat yellow snow

Buffeted by north
Winds our eyes find anchor in
Cold distant stillness

Do you think good Saint
Valentine enjoyed eating
This much chocolate

Stellar immersion
Baptism of faraway fire
Deep in winter's night

Who forgot to tell
Old Man Winter it's time to
Shift gears toward spring

Soft light warms our hearts
No matter what the distance
There's no place like home

Light lingers longer
On the western horizon
Nudging night backward

A solitary
Goose flies north pushing the clock
In our hearts forward

Deer don't know we're on
Daylight saving time now they
Spring ahead all year

A wet late snow weighs
On hearts more heavily than
Overmatched shovels

Translucent stillness
At dawn lets land sleep a spell
Under frost's blanket

Golden grass traces
Back to its source glowing on
Morning's horizon

Stealth green occupies
Acres it sneaked in last night
While we were asleep

Before beginning
Before the Let there be God's
Silence is awake

Father of Waters
You infuse the heartland with
Animating strength

Mother Nature gets
The last laugh says the farmer
He is not joking

Farmers work hard walk
Humbly and pray for enough
Water and sunshine

Gibbous moon shines holes
Through high passing clouds as a
Beagle bays below

Old roosters crow sure
Sun rises because they crow
Post hoc fallacy

When it comes to spring
Cleaning I'm with nature I
Abhor a vacuum

Pig manure ranks right
Up there on olfactory
Obnoxiousness charts

Father of waters
You flood banks and minds with spring
Sandbag memories

Yale played carillon
Bells that sweet April night we
Became Whiffenpoofs

Morning's glory climbs
The lattice-work of heaven
Entwining our hearts

Oxygen always
Finds a way to hearts and minds
Enjoy the freshness

With passage of time
Skin thins stretches sags but still
Sings in joy at touch

Tender transition
To shared sleep is a treasure
Beyond reckoning

We were surprised the
Old match lit on the first try
But it worked just fine

Incandescent bulbs
Can't hold a candle to the
Light of God within

Heartlanders see rain
Coming long before it's time
To close the windows

We celebrate spring's
Fresh start with the rhythmic song
Of windshield wipers

Worms inching toward
High ground move by feel not sight
That sounds familiar

When we're loving and
Just and not just loving our
Children gain balance

Grandma said Hector
Was a pup so long ago
There wasn't church yet

After listening
To long sermons our brains just
Start culling the heard

Sermons of even
Seventeen syllables can
Rile congregations

Huckleberry Finn
Speaks gospel truth in Twain's book
You can't pray a lie

If you wonder why
Heartlanders are cheerful please
See our sunrises

As golden syrup
Pours across farm fields we smell
Fresh morning pancakes

People obsessed with
Moving the needle often
Find hidden haystacks

Humility means
Thinking merely less often
Not less of ourselves

Eight point buck stares down
Cars while doe and fawn cross this
Rainy country road

Silence is sometimes
The most respectful response
We all can offer

Sister Colleen still
Anchors the radiance of
Faraway angels

Woodland sprites meet in
Mist mingling until dawn sings
Them back beneath bark

Bridging opposites
Is the job of love our hearts
Span many canyons

We harvest heartland's
Best crop when we plant seeds of
Peace within us all

Extraction of foot
From mouth is rarely graceful
Prevention is key

Ominous black sky
Winds swirl as lightning strikes land
Is this death's angel

Even a little
Light is enough to dispel
The deepest darkness

Weeds deserve respect
Despite fierce opposition
They certainly thrive

Our hearts ride every
Full moon across the night sky
Hitching our way home

They also serve who
Only stand and wait Milton
Didn't know airports

Backlit beauty of
Rolling heartland farm fields lifts
Our hearts at sunset

The most important
People in our lives may be
Least often mentioned

Her turtle shell hides
A heart far softer than I
Ever imagined

She sewed her own dress
Lovely blue silk with white trim
My dear Miss Wedgewood

Father of Waters
Your presence penetrates all
Heartland waterways

Gold medal divers
Enter the water without
So much as a splash

Good manners help us
Get through tired times by smoothing
The flow of feeling

A single whitetail
Bounds across the road into
Green sanctuary

Decibels count less
Out here silence softens sound
Like fireworks in fog

When we drill down deep
Enough right here in this place
We reach shared bedrock

What we share we square
Bliss is in our blood we can
Rise above the flood

Pure love fills that space
Where flowing hearts share sacred
Entrance and exit

Once upon a time
Septuagenarians
Seemed ancient creatures

Numbers on paper
Bring happiness or tears to
So many people

Moon monitors the
Distant lightning while wind whips
Waves across the lake

Odysseus saw
Rose-fingered dawn thousands of
Years later we do

When we make them friends
We destroy our enemies
Abraham Lincoln

I gave little bro
Scott a haircut and never
Got invited back

Back then Cub fans said
Hey anybody can have
A bad century

Gravity grounds us
Gives anchor but takes freedom
Until we can fly

Once I stood between
Two rumbling railroad cars and
Boogied to the beat

Be kind to badass
Septuagenarians
Legends in own minds

Geezer freak flags fly
At half mast we ruefully
Remember the mane

A beautiful beige
Carpet ripples in the breeze
Prairie grass blowing

Love lifts us all through
Seasons of severity
Light at tunnel's end

Soft bands of color
Support the rising moon 'til
Stars take the night shift

If we can't get stoked
About a sunrise it's time
To clear sinuses

We may see the same
Facts but differ about just
How much each fact weighs

Litmus tests often
Measure acidic levels
In testers themselves

Town folk seem surprised
To learn each stalk produces
Just one ear of corn

We all get to eat
Life insurance for lunch with
Organic farming

We will never be
More alive than when we give
Everything we have

Father of Waters
Your tributaries flow from
Every living realm

We serve justice best
When every breath lifts others
Toward what is right

Santa you have a
U.S. Marines ring just like
My Dad HOHOHO

Well Santa Claus served
In the Marines too Merry
Christmas HOHOHO

Facts came forth many
Years later but I'll always
Be grateful Dad fibbed

Wordless exchanges
Remind us that speech conveys
A fraction of truth

A bald eagle flew
Above us today heading
South across the lake

Aristotle said
Happiness is the purpose
The whole aim of life

Sunset and moonrise
Match tonight barnyard arches
Balance golden beams

A river runs through
The night sky a span that sparks
All eternity

Survival is not
The basis of progress it's
The other way round

I don't mean to sail
Into the cryptic but winds
Blow that way sometimes

We live in many
Worlds at once where our vision
Falls makes each world grow

Artists persuade paint
To reveal secrets that shine
Straight into our hearts

I can't always see
The moon but I can feel it
Back behind the clouds

In friendly fog we
May blunder fortunately
To surprise endings

Fifteen thousand shaves
Ago I lathered up and
Started scraping skin

Vanilla people
Live it up by adding some
Extra malt powder

Hell's angles may be
Acutely aware of their
Right to be obtuse

Love your enemies
Do good to them that hate you
Not much wiggle room

Cemetery stones
Outnumber the living in
Towns on the way down

Look if you had one
Shot one opportunity
Would you capture it

Drop the mic before
Dropping the body standing
Ovation awaits

Father of Waters
Your chocolate roiling churns
Hearts all around you

Earthquakes shake even
Bedrock blessed be the name
Giveth and taketh

Receiving is more
Blessed than giving sometimes
Let others' hearts flow

Magically there's
No distance from heart to heart
The miles don't matter

Upon a midnight
Clear out here we can see stars
Mirrored on water

Invisible pull
Of candle wicks mirrors the
Gravity of grace

Nana taught us that
Angels hide inside pockets
To watch over us

Our hidden helpers
Watch and wait for us to sing
Them into action

Maker of all things
Visible invisible
Guess that covers it

Bald eagle atop
This hill's tallest tree surveys
The kingdom below

Shafts of light fill the
Space where two voices shine in
Holy unison

Strong silent signal
Spreads sunshine or swirls dark smoke
We create our world

Heart strings tugged in jest
Recoil rarely ready to
Reach forth quite so far

Doc I've got a bad
Haiku habit seventeen
Syllables a day

There's usually
A puff of steam just before
The milk boils over

Keys to the kingdom
Rest within reach out of sight
But not out of mind

When waves pummel us
Clean in glorious sunshine
We feel the future

True cost of public
Life often exceeds the pay
Scale for name and fame

Guess what happens when
We turn off autocorrect
A lot less cussing

Cheerful acceptance
Of delayed fulfillment is
A mark of true grit

When subjunctive mood
Prevails should outweighs could and
Won't winds up winning

Our hearts sail on sky
The heartland's light blue ocean
Calls us home to you

Life etches lines in
Us as on stone water air
Air lines mean we're free

Grow from everything
Learning as much from loss as
Gain brings victory

Competition may
Develop character but
Clearly reveals it

Blowtorch brilliance burns
Holes through more arguments but
Kindness heals our wounds

Neighbors may object
But some socks feel better the
Second day they're worn

Blocks of silence build
Worlds of thought and things only
Dreamed of until now

Sky of grey gravel
Turns glorious gold as the
Sun inches upward

If what we love and
Do well helps others that's our
Natural best work

The first classic rock
And roll star was Sisyphus
Not Elvis Presley

Quietly shine love
In all directions until
The light passes on

Crimes clothed in smooth speech
Shine like a snake's skin before
It begins to molt

Who has dodged death and
Not wondered later about
Guardian angels

Even great loss brings
A blessed blanket of love's
Treasured memories

Tennis matches are
Battles but they are not war
Friends across the net

Softly luminous
That's what I'm talking about
Light without the heat

Forgiveness can't be
Forced waves of resentment fade
At rates of their own

Amends may arrive
Late like gifts forwarded from
An older address

Regret remains long
After opportunity's
Evaporated

Do tough talkers fear
The tenderness that flows from
Hearts of strong people

Stone-carved pronouncements
Write healthy conversation's
Early epitaph

Elders' heartfelt hymns
Fill us with peace and power
Even from afar

The glowing stone thrown
Into night's vast pond creates
High handsome halos

Simple lasts a lot
Longer than complicated
Fancy breaks down fast

He handed me my
Own advice and said it's time
For you to live it

Sanding and oiling
That unfinished furniture
Burnished both our hearts

Steady Sirius
Silent southeast lantern shines
Truth and consequence

Wise Mom to daughter
What he does will tell you much
More than what he says

Scholarly vandals
Correcting billboard grammar
For a higher clause

Socks without partners
Populate our planet still
Seeking reunion

Before long the stars
Will open our hearts and pour
Their light into us

Thank you for teaching
Us how to go beyond the
Boundaries of thought

Song spinning silence
Spirals blessing to the edge
Of the universe

Sadness dissipates
Like fresh February snow
Steaming in sunshine

Glass half empty or
Half full depends if we are
Drinking or pouring

Alexander the
Great conquered Socotra for
Its aloe vera

Being nobody
Living in the middle of
Nowhere opens doors

Reading people's minds
Is a skill mastered far less
Often than assumed

Thoughts are really gifts
To share with others and lift
Our level of love

Always guarding gold
Creates ice around our hearts
Freezing real assets

Most unintended
Consequences seem to bite
Us in the backside

Empty playground fills
With joyful children jumping
Rope to timeless rhyme

Beware the Ides of
March the old man said Caesar
Laughed and did not last

Quiet heroism
Lives on wherever people
Work for daily bread

One morning we will
Wake up and remember we've
Been here the whole time

Sacrificing life
For a living is trading
Diamonds for spinach

Think inside the bulb
Shadows all evaporate
Once light surrounds them

Just pick something great
To do and do it we get
Next what we think now

When do cows come home
Grandpa said we will cheer for
The Cubs until then

Messages get there
Even after our deadlines
Love has no limits

The correct answer
Is all of the above all
At once all the time

I am the eagle
Father of Waters' silent
Heartland rule flows on

About the Author

Lawrence Eyre taught and
Coached happily for decades
Deep in the heartland

Then haiku started
To strike like sneezing fits in
Hay fever season

An effective cure
For chronic haiku habits
Has yet to be found

 Born in Iowa along the Mississippi River, Lawrence Eyre holds a B.A. from Yale in American Studies. He has taught history and coached tennis for thirty years at Maharishi School in Fairfield, Iowa. The United States Professional Tennis Association named him national high school coach of the year in 2009.

Printed in June 2019
by Rotomail Italia S.p.A., Vignate (MI) - Italy